CONTENT

Hello, and Welcome to Christmas Sketchbook!

I hope that you will find this a useful resource when you're looking for new ways to tell the Christmas story where you are.

From short sketches to full-blown nativity plays, there is probably something in here to suit all shapes and sizes of churches or school groups.

Everything in this book has actually been performed by real people, in real places, and all amateurs! To accompany the scripts is a CD of specially written songs (plus some traditional carols) that have been found to work well in each context. For situations where there are no musicians handy we have provided backing tracks for you to use, even for the carols! And for situations where there are musicians we have included the top-line and chords for all the songs.

Most of these plays and songs were written at Altrincham and Purley Baptist churches where I had the privilege of working with some very gifted and enthusiastic people of all ages. These were big churches with lots of resources. My present church, Merstham Baptist, is a small (but perfectly formed) one, so I know what it's like when resources are limited.

I particularly want to mention Graham and Sally Jones from Purley. We did a number of productions together. Sally was wonderful at things like organising the children, making costumes and teaching dances and she always remembered the things that I forgot. Graham worked wonders with staging and curtains and special effects and props like megastars and wooden chariots. It was true teamwork and I hope that you also will experience that particular joy.

Of course you are free to add song choices or inspired ideas of your own. Obviously it's important that what you perform speaks clearly into your particular context; that's why all these were written!

God bless you and all your endeavors.
Happy Christmas!

Judy

ALL WRAPPED UP

BACKGROUND: This was performed for a group with learning difficulties. The relevant illustrations can be added at certain* points if desired. It's probably best to set the scene before it starts. The song 'All Wrapped Up' can be used before, during or after!

CAST: Two shepherds

THE SET: Not needed!

(Two shepherds, front facing, in a state of total shock)

A: Am I dreaming?

B: *(slowly)* No.

A: Did we really see angels then?

B: We did.

A: Have you ever seen angels before?

B: I have not.

A: They were big.

B: They were well big.

A: And scary.

B: Well scary.

A: But they didn't hurt us.

B: Phew. No, thank goodness.

A: What did they say?

B: They said… they said… "We're bringing you good news, about a Saviour, he's been born in your town and if you go and look for him you'll find him."

A: And we did, didn't we?

B: Little thing.

A: Little thing, all wrapped up.

B: All wrapped up, lying in a manger.

A: Yeah. Tell you what I don't get though…

B: What?

A: What's a saviour?

B: What's a saviour??

A: Yeah. The angel talked about him being a Saviour. Did he mean someone who puts his money in the bank?*

B: Eh? What you talking about? Oh… you mean a saver. No, that's not the same thing at all. What saviours do is they save people.

A: Oh… you mean like Superman?*

B: Well, sort of, yes. Saviours do rescue people…

A: So do firemen!* Is he like a fireman then?

B: Well yes, except that this particular Saviour is very special, because he's going to rescue people on the inside as well as the outside.

A: On the inside?! What does that mean?

B: Well, you see, we've got all kinds of mess on the inside of us, bad thoughts, bad memories, guilty secrets, everybody in the whole wide world needs saving on the inside. Yep. And that's what he's going to do.

A: But how can he? He's only a baby.

B: Yeah, but babies grow up you know…

A:	Oh yeah.		A:	Yeah. Blimey. No wonder the angels are excited!
B:	AND… you know who this baby is don't you?		B:	(*Getting up*) Better tell the Mrs.
A:	Err…		A:	Better had then. (*Exit*)
B:	He's the Son of God… that's who. He can do anything.			

THE END

* *

ANGEL VOICES

BACKGROUND: This nativity was originally acted entirely by children, but could be adapted.

CAST: 'Junior' angels: Helion, Santey, Aniya, Orlan - speaking parts for older children | Gabriel, the Archangel… should be a tall child (good actor) or an adult | Mary, Joseph, Elizabeth, Shepherds and Wise Men are all non-speaking parts | 4+ Toddler angels and/or 'stars' | Readers, singers, musicians or backing tracks.

THE SET: This was quite a challenge, but was eventually put up by a friendly scaffolding firm. It was a raised centre platform (Heaven) with stairs on both sides and space underneath for a stable area tall enough for children to stand (Earth!). The raised platform had a railing for Health and Safety reasons but it worked well as something the children could lean their elbows on and peer over to watch the action below. We draped fabrics over the whole thing, as one does. The other main thing needed is something that looks like a very big trumpet or horn. We (Graham) made one. Also, lots and lots of shiny gold and silver fabric for angel costumes of all sizes, various props for scene 2 and the ubiquitous manger of course!

Background music prior to start

SCENE 1: *Upper Stage*
(*'Junior' angels are crouched down on upper stage, out of sight at first*)

Background music fades
Blackout
Lights come up on set.
Singers to one side of stage

SONG: *Angel Voices (Verse 1 only)*

Music fades

HELION: (*Standing*) Right. Now we need to pick it up. Santey, you get the end and Aniya get the middle.

SANTEY: Ooooo…. it's heavy.

ANIYA: It's slithery as well.

HELION: That's because Orlan polished it so hard. Are you ready? One, two, three…

(*They lift a huge trumpet up, parallel with front stage*)

SANTEY: Now what?

HELION: We need Orlan to try it out (*Shouts*) Orlan!!!

ANIYA: He won't be able to blow it as hard as Gabriel.

HELION: I know, but we've got to make sure it works!!

(*Orlan comes running up stairs*)

ORLAN: Here I am. Hey. That is one cool trumpet.

HELION:	We want you to test it.
ORLAN:	I won't be able to blow it as hard as Gabriel.
SANTEY:	We know that.
ANIYA:	But we've got to make sure it works!
ORLAN:	O.K. then. I'll have a go.

(He puts his mouth to mouthpiece and blows. Squeaky trumpet noise off stage)

HELION:	Oh dear.
ORLAN:	I told you!!
HELION:	Try again.
SANTEY:	Yes, blow with all your might.
ANIYA:	Pretend you're an archangel!

(He blows again, this time the sound is much louder. Gabriel enters stage right)

HELION:	That's more like it!
GABRIEL:	(Gently chiding) What's all the noise about? (They stand to attention) What are you up to now? That's a trumpet. Where did it come from?
SANTEY:	Well Sir, we made it.
GABRIEL:	Did you now? (Looks it over) And a very fine trumpet it is too. What's it for?
HELION:	Well we thought, that… well, you know how the Lord told us that he's going down to the earth?
GABRIEL:	Yes.
HELION:	Well you see we thought that you could blow this when he's actually arriving.
ORLAN:	Make everyone jump.
ANIYA:	Er no, not exactly, more like…
SANTEY:	Like an announcement…
GABRIEL:	Oh I see. Now I understand. Unfortunately though, I can't use it.

OTHERS:	Ohhh…
GABRIEL:	Because… he's going to earth very quietly this time.
OTHERS:	Oh/What?/Why?
GABRIEL:	Well, he's going to be born as a human, a baby. And I don't think a baby would like that blown in its ear, do you?
HELION:	As a baby? You mean a little, tiny…?
GABRIEL:	Yes. Incredible isn't it?
ORLAN:	So he'll have to have… a mother.
GABRIEL:	Well spotted, Orlan.
HELION:	Who is it? Does she know?
GABRIEL:	Not yet. As a matter of fact, I'm just going to tell her. You can watch.
SANTEY:	So you won't be needing the trumpet then?
GABRIEL:	(As he descends the stairs) Not this time thank you. But don't lose it. It's going to come in handy one day.

READING: Luke 1 v 26-33 or 26-40.
(During this enter Mary, lower stage. She kneels when she sees Gabriel. Gabriel should raise his arms when his words are read. Towards the end of the reading Gabriel exits)

Mary crosses lower stage and greets Elizabeth. They do a simple dance movement during the song

SONG: Magnificat
(Solo, plus singers)

Mary and Elizabeth exit

SCENE 2: Upper Stage

HELION:	We haven't got much time!
SANTEY:	What do you mean?
HELION:	Well if Jesus is going to be born on earth we need to make

somewhere ready for him; somewhere really special and very beautiful. Now, what have we got?

(Turns round and starts picking things up and piling them into the arms of Orlan. Santey does the same with Aniya. Beautiful fabrics, golden jugs, bowls etc)

HELION/SANTEY: This would be good. Oooo and this. What about these? Yes that's lovely. And we must have some of these. They smell nice. Mmm. *(Etc, etc)*

ANIYA: My arms are aching.

SANTEY: How can your arms be aching? You're an angel.

ANIYA: Yes but I'm only a little angel.
(She and Orlan have their back to steps so don't see Gabriel coming up the steps behind them)

ORLAN: If you were Gabriel you could hold loads more than that. Loads and loads and…

GABRIEL: Did someone mention my name?

ORLAN: Oh whoops.

GABRIEL: It's alright. Now what are you up to?

HELION: We're getting ready to make a beautiful birthplace for the Lord.

GABRIEL: Oh. Oh dear. Oh dear oh dear.

ORLAN: What's the matter? Have we done something wrong?

GABRIEL: Not wrong exactly. It's just that… well the place where he is born is not to be beautiful. He doesn't want special treatment. He wants to be like everyone else on earth.

HELION: Like everyone else? But he's God.

GABRIEL: I know. But that's what he said. He's very surprising sometimes. Look, *(Pointing down at Mary and Joseph who are approaching the stage)* there's

Mary and Joseph. They're nearly at Bethlehem. That's where the Lord is going to be born.

SANTEY: Why Bethlehem?

GABRIEL: Because it was foretold. Everything the Lord foretold will come true. It always does. They won't find anywhere to stay. There's a census being taken and the town is packed.

ANIYA: Oh no!

SONG: *No Room*
(Singers)

On the Lower Stage people appear bustling about carrying bedding etc., innkeepers shaking their heads during the song. The song is followed by a reading during which Mary and Joseph settle in the area under the Upper Stage and a baby is discreetly produced while backs are turned to the audience!

READING: Luke 2 v 4-7
(Best as voice off-stage)

CAROL: *Away In A Manger (Verse 1 only)*
Stars, (little toddlers) walk onto sides of stage during this

SCENE 3: *Upper Stage*

ORLAN: Is it me, or is the universe extra specially starry tonight?

HELION: Yes! All the stars are coming out to shine.

SANTEY: Look how twinkly they are!

GABRIEL: The universe is very, very happy tonight.

ANIYA: *(to Helion)* What's that one?

SANTEY: Which one?

ANIYA: That one up there. *(Pointing directly overhead)*

HELION: I don't know. I've never seen it before.

GABRIEL:	Do you notice something special about it?
ORLAN:	Oh wow. It's right over where Jesus is.

SONG: *Shine On, Jesus*
Stars wander off at end

SCENE 4: *Upper Stage*

SANTEY:	I miss him not being in heaven.
ANIYA:	So do I.
HELION:	It won't be long till they realise who he is and then all sorts of people will want to meet him.
ORLAN:	You bet.
SANTEY:	Shouldn't we get a big red carpet ready?
HELION:	Great idea! There's one right here! Look, you grab the other end.

(They pick up a roll of carpet. Helion looks at Gabriel who is shaking his head)

	What? Can't we do this either?
SANTEY:	We can't do anything!!
GABRIEL:	Oh yes you can! You've got a very special job to do.
ANIYA:	What? What?
GABRIEL:	You're going to sing!
HELION:	But we're always singing.
GABRIEL:	This time you're going to sing with me… on earth.
ORLAN:	On earth? Oh wow. And will they hear us?
GABRIEL:	Oh, quite definitely. They'll see you as well. Look, there they are. Those shepherds.

(Shepherds come on)

HELION:	Shepherds? We're singing to shepherds? But aren't they poor and smelly? Nobody likes them.
GABRIEL:	The Lord likes them. He loves them as a matter of fact. Come on. We're going to tell them all about him.
SANTEY:	You mean, they'll be the first to know? He's being surprising again isn't he?
GABRIEL:	He certainly is.

(Gabriel runs down stairs and goes to stand over shepherds, arms raised)

READING: Luke 2 v 8 -1
(At the words "and suddenly", lots of little angels run on, and the 'junior' angels come down to join them. Singers start song immediately)

SONG: *Glory to God or We Sing Glory*

READING: Luke 2 v15
(Music fades away. Little angels exit and junior angels go back upstairs during reading. The shepherds walk to the front of the Lower Stage)

SCENE 5:

ORLAN:	Was that good or was that good!
HELION:	It was exciting!
ANIYA:	Did you see their faces?
SANTEY:	They were scared stiff!
ORLAN:	They won't ever forget tonight.
HELION:	Never ever.
ANIYA:	They'll tell all their friends…
SANTEY:	Over and over again…

SONG: *Nobody Loves Us*
(Shepherds sing along with singers)

SCENE 6:

HELION:	Jesus is making people happy already and he's only just been born!
GABRIEL:	He won't make everyone happy.

7

SANTEY: Why not?

GABRIEL: Well, not everyone will understand. Not everyone will want to worship him.

ANIYA: Why?

GABRIEL: All sorts of reasons. Some people worship other things, other people. Some people are too proud to worship anything.

HELION: Oh… But he's wonderful.

GABRIEL: Yes, we know that. We've seen him as he is. But to some people he'll just be… well, a nuisance.

ALL: A nuisance!?

ORLAN: O man! Human beings! They're so stupid sometimes!

GABRIEL: Not all of them. Look there.

(Pointing at Wise Men approaching from the back of the hall)

Centuries from now those three will be known as the three wise men.

Enter Wise Men, walking slowly. As the song is sung they make their way to the manger and kneel before it

SONG: *What Can We Bring?*

SCENE 7: *Upper Stage*

HELION: They're kneeling down. They know. How do they know?

GABRIEL: God the Father told them.

ANIYA: They've brought presents.

SANTEY: There's gold, that's because he's a King. What are the other two?

GABRIEL: Well there's frankincense, that's to do with him being holy… And there's myrrh. That's what you put on someone's body when they've died.

ORLAN: Well that's stupid. He's not going to die.

GABRIEL: I'm afraid he is. He'll be murdered by people who hate him.

ALL: *(Shout!)* No!

HELION: He can't die! He's God.

GABRIEL: I know. But he has a human body. That will die.

SANTEY: Will it hurt?

GABRIEL: Yes. A lot.

HELION: I can't bear it! Why? Why does he have to?

GABRIEL: Well, the thing is… it's all part of the plan. He's going to die to save them, so that they can be in heaven too. He's got to do it, it's the only way, but the good news is…

ORLAN: What?

GABRIEL: He'll come back to life again.

ALL: Yes!! Hurrah!!!

GABRIEL: And, he'll come back to heaven again.

ALL: Hurrah!!!!

GABRIEL: But that's a long way off. In the meantime we must do what we always do.

HELION: What? Go on missions you mean?

GABRIEL: Well, there's that, but what's the main thing we do?

SANTEY: We worship him.

GABRIEL: Yes. We worship him.

Everyone comes on stage and kneels at the crib during the song

SONG: *Angel Voices*

THE END

(This is a gentle ending. You could always use It's The Greatest Story as an encore)

* *

LOVE COME DOWN

BACKGROUND: This is a very simple nativity, which can be done with a small cast. It was written for a situation where rehearsal time was limited and it involved very little learning of lines. We used an adult as the Narrator, and children played the rest of the parts. Three young people played and sang. We performed it in the round, with no set and a minimum of props.

THE CAST: Narrator, Reader, the Angel Gabriel, Mary and Joseph, Roman Soldier, Innkeeper(s), Shepherds, Angels, Wise Men, Singer and musicians

---

SONG: *Love Is Coming*

NARRATOR: *(Quiet music over this is effective)*
Long, long ago, was love.
Love made the moon, the stars, the sun;
Love made the earth and everything in it.
Love loved all that was made, and called it good.
Love had a name, Love's name.. was God.
And people lived with God and lived in love,
In Paradise, we call it now.
But then in time, they turned, they fell,
They slipped away from love, and love was lost.
Not lost and gone, you understand,
But lost and hard to find.
And years and years and years went by.
Some searched for love,
From time to time you heard them sigh and say
Please come back love, come back
Please come again.
And then, one day…
Love came.

Enter Mary with a broom, sweeping, as music fades.
Angel Gabriel enters opposite her.

READER: 'Long ago God sent the angel Gabriel to the town of Nazareth in Galilee with a message for a virgin named Mary. She was engaged to Joseph from the family of King David.'

(Mary drops her broom.)

(This next section can be spoken by the angel if the angel can learn the lines!)

"Hello Mary", he said. "Don't be afraid! The Lord is pleased with you. You are truly blessed! You're going to have a son. His name will be Jesus. He will be great and will be called the Son of God Most High."

NARRATOR: Mary wondered how this could happen, but the angel told her that nothing was impossible with God. His promises always, always come true. *(Exit Angel)*

(Mary kneels as song is sung)
SONG: *God Has Chosen Me*

NARRATOR: Mary was going to be married to Joseph.

(Enter Joseph. He needs to stand away from Mary with his arms folded)

When he found out that she was going to have a baby, he was really upset. He didn't want to hurt Mary's feelings so he decided to call off their wedding quietly. But God sent an angel to him as well.

(Enter Angel. The following lines can be spoken by the angel also)

"Joseph," said the angel. "Don't be afraid to get married to Mary. The baby in her is from the Holy Spirit. It's a boy!

When he is born call him Jesus. It means Saviour. He's going to save people from the mess they've got into."

SONG: *Love Is Coming*
(During which Angel leaves and Joseph goes to Mary and takes her by the hand)
Drum roll. Enter Roman soldier

ROMAN SOLDIER: Quiet everyone! Quiet! Listen to me!

(Reading from a scroll)

I am bringing an order from his Excellency Caesar Augustus:
"Every man, woman and child in this region must return to their family home to be counted. This order must be obeyed!"

NARRATOR: Mary and Joseph had to leave Nazareth and go to Bethlehem

(Joseph and Mary do a circuit round the room during this dialogue)

because that's where his family had come from. So they set off on the long journey south. It was nearly time for the baby to be born. But when they got to Bethlehem it was full of people, packed.

(Start playing and singing)
SONG: *No Room*
(Narration continues loudly over the top)

And there was no-where to stay. Not a room to be had. All the inns were full of people who had come to be counted. Joseph knocked on all the doors but it was no good.

(Wait for song to end)

In the end, they found a bit of shelter by a feeding trough, and there, among the animals and the hay, the Saviour of the world was born.

(Baby secreted under blanket in crib! Mary cradles it/him)

CAROL: *Away In A Manger (Verse 1 only)*

READER: Luke 2:7

'Mary gave birth to her first-born child, a son. She wrapped him in strips of cloth and laid him in a manger because there was no room for them in the village inn.'

(Mary puts baby back in crib)

During this, some distance away from Joseph and Mary, some shepherds appear, shielding their eyes)

NARRATOR: Meanwhile, on the hills outside Bethlehem a most amazing thing happened. Some shepherds were looking after their sheep when suddenly there was a great noise

(Synthesizer choral sounds and other sfx throughout this)

and a really bright light and there they were - thousands of angels, and all singing "Glory to God in the highest!"

(Gabriel and Angels of various sizes, as available, come on facing shepherds)

Then an angel spoke to the shepherds…

(The following can be read by the Narrator or a reader)

ANGEL: Don't be afraid! I have some good news for you, which will make everyone very happy. This very day in King David's hometown a Saviour has been born for you. He is Christ the Lord. You will know who he is, because you will find the baby wrapped in strips of cloth and lying in a manger."

(Angels drift away. Music fades)

NARRATOR: Then all the angels faded away and the stars shone brightly in the sky. The shepherds looked at each other in amazement. "Wow. We've just seen angels!" they said. Come on! Let's go into town and find the baby."

(Shepherds cross stage and cluster round the crib looking at the baby)

SONG: *Shine On, Jesus*

NARRATOR: And there were Wise Men who came to see Jesus. They had come a long, long way from another country following a special star that they saw in the sky.

(Enter Wise Men carrying gifts and pointing at imaginary star)

READER: Matthew 2: 9b -11
The star went before them until it stopped over the place where the child was. When the wise men saw the star, they were filled with joy. They went to the house where the child was and saw him and his mother, Mary.

(The wise men act this out)

They bowed down and worshipped the child. They opened gifts they had brought for him. They gave him treasures of gold, frankincense and myrrh.

NARRATOR: *(Quiet music over this)*
Strange presents for a child, you might think, but this was not any child. This was the Son of God. Gold was for a King, frankincense for someone holy, and myrrh was for someone who would suffer and die. Jesus was holy, perfect in fact, and he did suffer and die, but he was raised from the dead and now he is King Jesus, Lord of Lords and King of Kings in fact, reigning over this whole enormous Universe. And that is why we tell his story every Christmas, the story of love, love come down, love come down to save us.

CAROL: *O Come, Let Us Adore Him*
(3 verses, sung by all)

THE END

* *

MY MASTER'S HALL
An all-age nativity

BACKGROUND: This nativity has a strongly medieval flavour, and wherever possible the music is actual 16th century music, or written in the style of! You could perform this as part of a banquet, with tables, food et al, but we went for something simpler.

THE SET: We used the length of our church, with two raised 'thrones' at one end, the choir to one side of the thrones and the audience seated down the sides of the church. The action all took place up and down the centre space.

THE CAST: Narrator 1, Narrator 2, Man, Boy and Girl, Satan, Readers, Mary, Gabriel, Dancers, Joseph, Shepherds, Angels, Wise Men | Only the narrators and readers are speaking parts | A Lord and Lady seated on the thrones. (Optional) | We used an adult choir this time, and appropriate instruments, but children of all ages were involved in the actual acting. The Choir dressed in medieval costumes.

Lights down
Musical introduction
Lights up on choir

SONG: *Welcome*

Bell shimmer and rain-stick (Passage of time)
Lights to centre
(There is a mime during the following narration. A tall figure, representing God, and a small boy and girl representing man and woman enter at one end and walk slowly hand in hand through the centre space)

NARRATOR 1: Long, long ago, when the world was not so old, God walked with man as a man walks with a friend. Man obeyed God and God provided for man and for a while everything was good and all was well.

(A cowled figure appears at the side holding a bowl of golden fruit and the children turn to look)

NARRATOR 2: Until one day, greed reared its ugly head.

NARRATOR 1: And man was tempted and man gave in, disobeying his God.

(Children let go of mans hand and take fruit from bowl, then wander back the way they came. The God-figure stares after them.)

Their friendship was broken; their peace was shattered. Sin had entered the world and mankind's trouble began.

(God-figure exits in opposite direction to the children.)

NARRATOR 2: But God still loved his world, and longed to restore it to himself. Over the centuries he spoke through the prophets of a Saviour who would come one day and make peace between God and man.

READING: *Isaiah 9: 2, 6*

NARRATOR 1: Watch now, my Lords and Ladies. Watch now as God's promise is fulfilled.

(During the following Mary enters to centre and Gabriel comes to meet her from opposite end. Mary kneels down before the angel until after the reading)

Choir sing
CAROL: *The Angel Gabriel (Verse 1 only)*

READER: *Luke 1:26-33, 38*

Exit Gabriel
Music, dancers come on and dance round Mary or with her during song.
Mary could sing, or a soloist from the choir.

SONG: *Magnificat*

Exit dancers. Enter Joseph from opposite end to Mary.

NARRATOR 2: Now see, here's Joseph. Joseph was the man Mary was to marry. When he heard what had happened to her he was torn. He didn't know what to do;

(Joseph flops down to his knees and then flat on the floor. Enter Angel, standing with arms lifted over Joseph)

but an angel came to him as well, in a dream, and said…

READER: *Matthew 1: 20b-21*
Exit Angel

NARRATOR 1: When Joseph woke up

(Joseph gets up and goes to Mary, taking her hand)

he did what the angel commanded him and took Mary home as his wife.

(Drum roll, lighting change onto Roman soldier on the stage. He reads from a scroll)

ROMAN SOLDIER: Hear ye, hear ye. By order of his Excellency Caesar Augustus I hereby give notice of the Roman census. Each man, woman and child must return to the home of their family to be registered and taxed. This order must be obeyed!

NARRATOR 2: Joseph's family had come from Bethlehem, so that was where he and Mary had to go. They set off on their long journey.

(You need to improvise 'a long journey' with your available space)

For seventy miles they travelled, until they came to Bethlehem.

(A manger containing' Baby Jesus' well concealed in straw is placed in the centre space and Mary and Joseph make their way towards it)

NARRATOR 1: But Bethlehem was full, there was nowhere to stay, and Mary's baby was ready to be born, so they settled in a sheltered place, and there in all the dust and dirt, Jesus, the Son of God was born.

(Mary picks up and cradles baby during the next song)

(Choir Sing)
SONG: *The Saviour Of The World Is Born*
(Tune: I Saw Three Ships)

Song ends
Lights on shepherds, who are positioned some distance from Mary and Joseph.

READER: *Luke 2: 8-14. (LB)*
(During this reading Gabriel appears to the shepherds and is joined by all the little angels.)

SONG: *God Rest Ye Merry Gentlemen*
(Only the verse beginning 'From God our heavenly Father)
(The angels and the shepherds walk round the manger at this point and then settle somewhere nearby. Instrumental music continues until all are settled)

READER: *Luke 2:20*

NARRATOR 2: And all the things that they had heard were just as ancient prophets said, and more, and more, God's master plan drawn up before the world began, seen now by humble sons of men… these eyes have seen salvation come.

READER: *Matthew 2: 1, 2*

SONG: *We Three Kings*
(Enter the Kings who process very slowly to the manger during this)

READER: *Matthew 2:9b-11*
(After presenting gifts Kings kneel.)

NARRATOR 1: My Lords and Ladies, our story does not end here. The child you see in this manger will grow into a man, a man who will heal the sick, feed the hungry, save the lost, and raise the dead.

NARRATOR 2: A man who will be loved and hated, welcomed and shunned. A man who will die in our place, for he is the 'Lamb of God who takes away the sin of the world.'	**ALL:** Amen
NARRATOR1: My Lords and my Ladies. This man is risen from the dead and is now enthroned in heaven: your true Lord, your true Master; forever and forever.	*Cast and Choir straight into…* **SONG:** *Gaudate* *(This is repeated until all the cast is assembled. The last 'Gaudate' should be a worshipful shout with hands and heads lifted to heaven)* **THE END**

*　*

SANTA & NODDY

BACKGROUND: This is a two-hander and needs good actors to carry it off

THE CAST: Santa is very theatrical, larger than life. He has an enormous ego needing constant propping up by a very old Noddy, a Clive Dunn type in terms of voice and mannerisms but with a lot more savvy.

THE SET: You will need a sofa, a small desk/table, a stool and a free-standing mirror (or a large mirror on a wall). We went for a very Victorian Christmas sort of look, chaise-longue etc.

Enter Santa carrying hat. Walks to mirror

SANTA: Noddy!! Confound the boy! Where is he?

(Puts on hat, admires himself from all angles)

Oh yes… Noddy! One is waiting… Mm… splendid. Ho-ho-ho. Ho-ho-ho.

(Enter Noddy, hunched over, with stick and bag of letters.)

NODDY: Sorry Santa, it's me legs. I'm not as young as I was you know.

SANTA: Nonsense, boy. You're a mere hundred and eight, whereas I…

NODDY: Hundred and nine.

(Slumps at table, sorting letters into piles)

SANTA: Hundred and nine then, whereas I, I, Noddy, am one hundred and thirty-five! Mind you, I am… somewhat exceptional. One doesn't like to boast Noddy but few, very few, if indeed any at all *(lapsing into Churchillian)* have ever, in the field of human endeavour accomplished anything like…

NODDY: *(Interrupting)* You're not really human though.

SANTA: You're right Noddy! You're SO right! Out of the mouths of babes… One is, in fact, Superhuman. Oh yes.

NODDY: That's it.

SANTA: You know Noddy, people just don't get it do they? They have no idea.

NODDY: *(Bored)* No idea. No.

SANTA: No conception of the work involved. The hours of planning, the wrapping and labelling, the wretched reindeer, all that frightful ducking and diving under the flight path, over the flight path, the soot, the dry

14

cleaning bills, the endless mince pies and appalling cheap sherry. I tell you Noddy, if they only knew, they might be a little more… *(sob)* … grateful.

NODDY: No, no, they are grateful Santa.

SANTA: I just feel so… taken for granted sometimes.

NODDY: Taken for granted? Not you Santa.

SANTA: This will shock you, Noddy, but sometimes I feel like packing the whole thing in… I don't know… writing my memoirs… spending more time with the reindeer.

NODDY: But you hate the reindeer. Santa, come on now. Think of the children.

SANTA: *(Malevolently)* I am thinking of the children

NODDY: All those innocent little faces…

SANTA: Yerss.

NODDY: Just waiting for you to come along and fill their stockings…

SANTA: Pillowcases.

NODDY: Pillowcases then. It's your public, Santa. Know what I mean? You've got a duty to your public. The show must go on annat!

(Slight pause. Change of tack)

They all think the world of you, you know.

SANTA: Do they? Do they really and truly?

NODDY: Oh yes. Christmas wouldn't be Christmas without you, Santa.

SANTA: Do you think so?

NODDY: I know so. In fact, you are Christmas as far as Joe Public is concerned.

SANTA: Do you know Noddy, I think you're right. It is, after all, one's destiny.

NODDY: That's it! Destiny. That's it.

SANTA: Duty calls and I shall obey.

NODDY: You shall, Santa.

SANTA: Onward, ever onward.

NODDY: *(Getting bored with this now)* Yes, yes.

SANTA: Nil desperandum, old friend.

NODDY: Yes, alright then! Now can we do the letters?

SANTA: Letters? Letters?

NODDY: It's the …* today Santa. *(*Insert actual date)*

SANTA: Is it, by Jove?

NODDY: Only…* days to go. *(*Insert no. of days till 25th)*

SANTA: Good heavens! Let's get to it then. Ledger! *(Noddy hands it to him)* Pen! *(Ditto)* Fire away dear boy.

(In this section you need to insert whatever gifts are fashionable at the time and perhaps use the names of local people who will be known to your audience)

NODDY: Right. Dear Santa, I want a _____ and _____

SANTA: I want! Whatever happened to 'please may I?'

NODDY: Modern youff, Santa… and a _____ From _____

SANTA: *(Sigh)* Next.

NODDY: This is from _____ Dear Santa, please, please may I…

SANTA: How nice.

15

NODDY:	… please may I have ____ and any spare millions you might have stashed away.
SANTA:	Huh!!
NODDY:	Dear Santa, oh… it's one of those.
SANTA:	What? Not a parking fine… how dare they!!
NODDY:	No, it's one of those funny ones. 'Ere. It says 'Dear Santa, I don't know if you can help but what I want most is my Dad to come home and my Mum to stop crying. Please do your best.' *(Pause)*
SANTA:	Oh really! I do wish they wouldn't.
NODDY:	Shall I put it in this pile?
SANTA:	I suppose so. Is it my imagination Noddy, or is that pile getting bigger every year?
NODDY:	I think you're right Santa.
SANTA:	Never mind. Continue.
NODDY:	Dear Santa, I'd like a Ferrari please. Any kind. Thanks a lot, your pal _____
SANTA:	Ah yes, good old greed. You know where you are with greed.
NODDY:	Dear Santa, Please can you stop the bad people putting bombs in our city and shooting people. From Jasmine.
SANTA:	You see greed is such a simple thing. I want and therefore I absolutely must have.
NODDY:	*(Sigh)* Dear Santa, My Mum says all she wants for Christmas is for everyone in our house to stop arguing for five minutes. Can you do miracles?
SANTA:	*(Exploding)* No! I cannot do miracles. What is the matter with these children? Why do they keep asking the impossible? It never used to be like this.

NODDY:	Ah. Well. Times have changed, Santa
SANTA:	Once upon a time it was so straightforward. I supplied all the goodies but miracles were fairly and squarely in the hands of…
NODDY:	God.
SANTA:	Precisely.
NODDY:	Ah but you see, it's all very confusing nowadays. Children hear all kinds of old baloney about God. I don't think they know what to believe in anymore. I suppose they think they might as well give you a try.
SANTA:	Eh? Well it's all a great embarrassment. I wish they wouldn't. One does know one's limitations, Noddy. Great and exceptional as I am, certain things are most definitely beyond me. Don't believe? Good heavens. Can't they see? It's as plain as the nose on poor old Rudolf. I suppose they'll stop believing in me next!!! Ha-ha ha-ha-ha-ha.

(Forced laughter from both, suddenly shudders to a halt)

	Lets leave the letters for now.
NODDY:	Are you sure Santa?
SANTA:	Mm. It all seems strangely pointless all of a sudden.
NODDY:	Oh dear, oh dear. You can't say that. What about 'Peace and Goodwill to all men?'
SANTA:	Exactly! What if there isn't any?
NODDY:	Eh? Well… I dunno… doesn't bear thinking about.
SANTA:	*(Subdued)* No.
NODDY:	Nah. You're just tired, that's all.

SANTA:	Maybe so, dear boy, maybe so. I think I shall go and lie down for a while. Bring me a large glass of something would you? (*Walks to exit*)	NODDY:	And a plate of mincers Santa? (*Follows him to exit*)
		SANTA:	And a plate of your very best mince pies.

THE END

* *

STAR

BACKGROUND: No prizes for guessing the central theme of this nativity play! You will need some children who can learn lines and act well, and one of them (Susie) needs to be able to sing well also. A man who can do a 'Mr Kipling' voice is needed for the voice of the star. He can read his lines into a microphone off-stage.

THE CAST: Apart from the 'Star' voice, all are children | Laura, Susie, Charlie, Katie are all school children (8-11) | Angel Gabriel: speaking part | Mary, Joseph, Villagers, Shepherds, Angels, Wise Men: non-speaking | A choir | A band, with a synthesiser, or backing tracks

THE SET: The set can be very ordinary apart from 'The Star,' which needs to have something of a wow factor. Graham made ours from a wooden frame, aluminium foil and loads of fairy lights. It was suspended high behind thick curtains at the rear of the stage and the lights on it were switched on as the curtains were pulled back. The audience, sitting in the dark, gasped audibly! You will also need a couple of stage blocks and a manger.

Front stage empty. Rear curtains closed. Lights down.
A few bars of music and lights up. Four children come in from stage left in school uniform. They are arguing on the way home from school.

LAURA:	I hate you Susie Jones! You got me into trouble again!
SUSIE:	I don't care.
LAURA:	You're mean and nasty!
SUSIE:	So?
CHARLIE:	What did she do?
LAURA:	She was talking in assembly and Miss told ME off.
SUSIE:	I wasn't!
KATIE:	You were Susie. Everybody knows.
SUSIE:	Well I don't care. I hate school. School's stupid.
CHARLIE:	You've got to go, Susie. Otherwise you can't get a job.
SUSIE:	I don't want a job. So there.
LAURA:	Well if you don't have a job you won't have any money. Duhhh!
SUSIE:	Yes I will! I'm going to be RICH!!!
EVERYONE:	How?
SUSIE:	I'm going to be… a star!
KATIE:	Oh yeah?
SUSIE:	Yes I am!!

SONG: *Great Big Star*
(*Performed by Susie*)

LAURA:	A great big star? I don't think so.

KATIE:	And you've certainly got a great big head!	**SUSIE:**	That's a funny name.
SUSIE:	Don't care.	**STAR:**	Do you think so?

KATIE: And you've certainly got a great big head!

SUSIE: Don't care.

(Laura, Katie and Charlie leave. Susie sits down and puts her head in her hands Charlie wanders back)

CHARLIE: Come on Susie. You're not allowed to walk home alone.

SUSIE: Don't care.

(Synthesiser noise …gradually getting VERY loud)

CHARLIE: What's that noise?

SUSIE: What?

CHARLIE: Can't you hear it?

SUSIE: Yeeees. It's scary. What is it? Ooooo save me!

(She grabs onto him. Curtain pulls back to reveal a huge and very dazzling star. Dry ice effect if possible. Music gradually dies down)

STAR: (Big booming voice) Hello Earthlings!! … I said 'Hello.' Are you non-speaking earthlings?

CHARLIE: Er… No.

STAR: Oh good.

CHARLIE: We were just a bit… s-s-s-surprised.

SUSIE: F-f-f-frightened, as a matter of fact.

STAR: Oh no need for that. I haven't exploded for a long time.

SUSIE: What are you?

STAR: What do I look like?

CHARLIE: Well, you look like… a star.

STAR: Well done sir!

SUSIE: What's your name?

STAR: My name is Ovwunda.

SUSIE: That's a funny name.

STAR: Do you think so?

SUSIE: Well I wouldn't really know. I've never met a star before.

CHARLIE: Why are you here?

STAR: Ah yes. Well. I'm on a mission you see. Haven't been sent on a mission for over two thousand years!

SUSIE: Two thousand years? You must be very old.

STAR: Oh I am. Millions and millions of years…

CHARLIE: (Interrupts) What sort of mission?

STAR: Oh. Well, apparently you're getting it all wrong.

CHARLIE: Getting what wrong?

STAR: Why, Christmas of course.

SUSIE: O I love Christmas. Presents and food… and food and presents…

STAR: That's just it you see. Those things are very nice but Christmas is actually a lot more important than that. Do you know the story?

CHARLIE: Kind of…

STAR: Well please may I tell it? I was there, you know.

SUSIE: There was a star in the story wasn't there? Were you it?

STAR: I was, young earthling! And in those days I was even twinklier than I am now!!

CHARLIE: Alright then. Tell us.

STAR: Well, a very, very, very long time ago The Maker…

CHARLIE: (To Susie) He means God. I think.

STAR: Hmmm… The Maker made the Universe. He made it

brilliantly, especially me of course, and he made it absolutely huge!! And he loved every bit of it, but most of all he loved… earthlings.

CHARLIE: (To Susie) Humans.

STAR: Yersss. And the earthlings loved him. And for a while everything in the garden was lovely but then things went wrong because the Maker had an enemy and the earthlings were tricked by him and they got themselves into a terrible mess and as time went by it got worse. They just wouldn't listen to the Maker you see. They nearly always wanted to do their own thing and it always got them into trouble. So in the end the Maker did something quite… extraordinary.

SUSIE: What?

STAR: He decided…

CHARLIE: What did he decide?

STAR: He decided to go to earth himself to sort them out once and for all. Of course he didn't go as he really is, that would have just flattened everybody and in spite of everything he still loved them. He's like that you see. No, he made himself into an earthling and he arrived as a weak, tiny, helpless little baby.

SUSIE: I know! You mean the baby Jesus, don't you?

STAR: Yes, that's right! That is his name.

CHARLIE: Oh. So, was he the Maker then?

STAR: Oh **yes**. That's the whole point! And not many people get it! Anyway, he sent an angel first, to a town called Nazareth in Israel. There was a young lady there called Mary. Oh look. Here they are. Quick. Get out of the way.

(Enter Mary and the Angel. Susie and Charlie go to side of the stage and observe from now on)

ANGEL: Hello Mary. Don't be afraid. God is well pleased with you and he's chosen you for something very special. You're going to have a baby and you are to call him Jesus. His Father will be the Most High God and he will be the Son of God. It's true Mary. Nothing is impossible with God.

(Angel leaves. Mary kneels)

STAR: Well. Mary was absolutely amazed and delighted by what the angel said; to think that the Maker had chosen her to be the Mother of Jesus!

SONG: *God Has Chosen Me (Choir solo)*

CHARLIE: Just a minute! Where's Joseph?

STAR: Ah… well… he was supposed to be getting married to Mary you see. Then when all this happened he thought maybe he shouldn't, but then he had a visit from an angel as well!! The angel told him to go ahead and marry her, so he did.

(Joseph comes in and takes Mary by the hand and leads her off stage left during this)

Anyway, time passed and the baby grew inside Mary and soon it was time for it to be born.

CHARLIE: Just a minute! They're in the wrong place. They're in Nazareth and the baby gets born in Bethlehem!

STAR: Quite right earthling. Well spotted. But as a matter of fact, they had to go to Bethlehem for a particular reason. They had to register in something called a census; it was the law. So off they went.

(Villagers enter from stage right doing lots of bustling about. Mary and Joseph come back in and head towards stage right)

It was a hard journey for Mary and when they got to Bethlehem it was packed out. Lots and lots of people had come to register from all over the place and could they find anywhere to stay?

SUSIE: No they couldn't!

SONG: *No Room*

(Semi-circle of figures. Mary and Joseph go to each one and they shake their heads during song. Everyone except J+M leave as song finishes)

STAR: And so, on this night of all nights, when there was absolutely nowhere to stay, the Maker, the Baby Jesus, was born into the world. Joseph bustled about to find some straw to keep them warm and he found a feeding trough for the baby to sleep in.

SUSIE: A feeding trough?

STAR: Oh you call it a manger don't you. *(Music comes up)* That's right. A manger.

CAROL: *Away In A Manger (Verse 1 only)*
(During this shepherds take up position)

CHARLIE: I've been thinking. It wasn't very posh, was it? I mean considering who the baby was.

STAR: No. But it was just the way he wanted it. He wanted to be seen with the poorest people. He wanted them to know that they were important to him. As a matter of fact, the first people to hear that he had been born were poor shepherds, out on the hills.

(Shepherds on stage to the side. The Angel appears and they fall to their knees)

They were visited by an angel, and they were very frightened at first, but the angel spoke to them.

ANGEL: Don't be afraid. I've got good news for you, really good news, for you and for everyone. Today, in Bethlehem, your Saviour has been born. He has arrived. This is how you'll know it's true. You will find a baby, all wrapped up and lying in a manger.

STAR: *(Music up)* And then lots more angels appeared, hundreds and thousands of them and they were all singing…

(Song as all angels come onto stage)

SONG: *Glory To God* or *We Sing Glory*

STAR: *(Angels leave stage now)* And then the angels all slipped away into heaven one by one and the shepherds just stood there staring at first. They couldn't quite believe it, that the angels had come to them, the people nobody liked, and given them a message from the Maker.

SUSIE: Why did nobody like them?

STAR: Oh. Well, they were very poor, you see, and they looked after sheep, day and night, so they were very, erm, very…

CHARLIE: Smelly?

STAR: They were very, very smelly.

SUSIE: Poor shepherds.

CHARLIE: Yeah. Poor shepherds.

STAR: Poor shepherds? Why they're the happiest, most excited bunch of shepherds you'll ever see in your life!

SONG: *Nobody Loves Us*
(Shepherds come to front of stage during intro to song. Choir sing it but shepherds can sing along/do actions)

STAR: And so they rushed off to Bethlehem to find the baby in a manger. That was the clue that he was a special baby you see. People don't put babies in feeding troughs! They knew that if they found one then everything the angels said was true!

(Shepherds gather round manger)

And look! They found him, just as the angel had said, and when they'd had a good look at him, they were so excited that they rushed off and told all their friends and neighbours.

(Shepherds rush off stage)

In the meantime, Mary quietly nursed her baby and thought about all these amazing things that were happening.

SONG: Shine On, Jesus

SUSIE: That song's about you!

STAR: Well, sort of. But it's more about Jesus really.

CHARLIE: But I thought you were in the East.

STAR: Oh, I was. I started in the East. But I moved. We do move, you know, us stars. But that time was special, by order of the Maker.

SUSIE: Why?

STAR: I was to guide someone to Jesus. Show them the way.

CHARLIE: I know! The Kings!

STAR: Yes. No. Well that's what some people call them but actually what they were was Wise Men.

Very educated. Knew where all the stars and planets were so when I appeared in the sky they guessed, quite rightly, that something special was happening. Someone had told them that one day a very special person would be born and a new star would appear at the same time. And so they followed me, all the way to Jesus.

CAROL: *We Three Kings*
(During this the wise men process in)

CHARLIE: So that's why you're called Ovwunda.

STAR: Precisely. I'm the star of wonder!

SUSIE: Is that the end of the story?

STAR: Gracious, no. It's just a part of it. Baby Jesus grew up into Man Jesus and did many wonderful things that only someone with the Maker's power and the Maker's love can do.

CHARLIE: But he was crucified wasn't he? They killed him!

STAR: Yes. It was terrible. The old Enemy you see, he and his agents. Tried to finish off The Maker once and for all. Thought he'd done it at first as well. Huh. Kill the Maker? The very idea! He did die… but he came back to life again. We knew he would! All the stars and planets were singing and dancing and there was…

SUSIE: Dancing?

STAR: Everybody worships him you see. He's wonderful. Doing all that… for you earthlings.

CHARLIE: I don't get it. Why does he love us so much?

STAR: Oh, why! He can't help himself. He's made of love you see. Mind you, millions of earthlings love him now. Mmm.

21

SUSIE:	If I talk to him can he hear me?	STAR:	No, no. I know that. What's this place called?
STAR:	Oh most certainly.	CHARLIE:	It's called ____
SUSIE:	Well, can I sing him a song?	STAR:	Oh. I've never been to a _____ before. Well, goodbye earthlings.
STAR:	Oh. He'd love you to sing him a song!		
SUSIE:	O.K. then.	CHOIR:	*Goodbye Star.*
SONG:	*Shine*	SUSIE:	No. Wait. Can we sing one more song before you go?
STAR:	Oh thank you! That was delicious. *(Sigh)* Well. It's time I was getting back into orbit. I hope I've remembered everything I was supposed to say. What did you say this place was called?	STAR:	Go on then. The universe can wait a minute or two. Strike up the band! Happy Christmas Earthlings!!!!!
		(Music)	
CHARLIE:	Planet earth.	SONG:	*It's The Greatest Story* Balloons etc

THE END

* *

THE BIG ONE

BACKGROUND: This sketch is best filmed if possible because of the freeze ending.

THE CAST: Represent a stereotypical middle class family; a man, his wife, their eleven year old son, and the visiting Auntie. | The atmosphere is rather strained.

THE SET: A family living room on Christmas Day.

There is a very large, beautifully wrapped present to the rear of the scene. We are halfway through opening presents.

HUSBAND:	*(Opening parcel)* Now what have we here? *(Golf socks)* Oh, marvellous - socks. Thank you, Auntie. They're splendid. Yes indeed.
AUNTIE:	I thought they'd go with your jumper.
HUSBAND:	*(No idea)* My jumper.
WIFE:	Your golfing jumper, darling.
AUNTIE:	The one I bought you last Christmas.
HUSBAND:	Oh, that jumper. Yes, of course! They'll set it off a treat.
WIFE:	You'll be the talk of the golf club.
HUSBAND:	Mmmm.
MATTHEW:	This doesn't work.
WIFE:	Has it got batteries?
MATTHEW:	Yes.
HUSBAND:	You've probably put them in the wrong way round Matthew.
MATTHEW:	*(Indignant)* No I haven't.

HUSBAND: (Patronising) Let's have a look shall we?

MATTHEW: (Loud sigh)

WIFE: (Opening present, holds up a big jumper) Oh, this is lovely darling.

HUSBAND: I thought you'd like it darling.

WIFE: Oh I do darling.

AUNTIE: It's miles too big.

WIFE: Oh I don't know…

AUNTIE: And it's not your colour at all.

WIFE: Well I think it's rather nice.

AUNTIE: I'd take it back if I were you.

HUSBAND: (Clears throat) More sherry, Auntie?

AUNTIE: Well if you insist.

WIFE: Any more under the tree?

HUSBAND: Afraid not. That's it for the presents.

MATTHEW: (Dramatically) Yes! T………ime for the Big One!

WIFE: Don't be silly dear.

MATTHEW: Oh please. Please can we open it?

HUSBAND: Open what Matthew? What are you talking about?

MATTHEW: (Gesticulating at the parcel behind him) It. You know.

HUSBAND: What is 'it'?

MATTHEW: This! This one! Here!

HUSBAND: There's nothing there.

WIFE: You're just imagining things darling.

MATTHEW: No I'm not. Look. (Bangs it) It's real (Bang, bang) Can't you see it?

AUNTIE: Has the boy gone mad?

HUSBAND: (Clears throat) What is it exactly that you can see Matthew?

MATTHEW: Is this a trick? It's a trick isn't it? Well…. It's a great big present wrapped up in sort of red and silver with dangly bits.

HUSBAND: (Sarcasm) Is it really?

WIFE: Matthew, stop. Now. That's quite enough.

AUNTIE: He's obviously over-excited.

MATTHEW: I'm going to open it then.

AUNTIE: There'll be tears before bedtime.

HUSBAND: He's showing off. Just ignore him.

WIFE: (Looking at watch) Oh look; time for the Queen.

(She goes to turn T.V. on. Matthew begins to tear wrapping off from the back of the carton, tears open the top and looks in)

HUSBAND: Another mince pie Auntie? They're exceptionally good this year my darling. Did you make them yourself?

AUNTIE: As if.

WIFE: Of course, my darling. (She's lying)

HUSBAND: Mince pie Matthew?

MATTHEW: (He is transfixed looking into the box. Pause)

Oh wow.

(Picks up a card and reads)

It says it's for all of us.

(They all turn to look at him. Freeze)

THE END

* *

23

THE CHRISTMAS TREE

THE CAST: Sophie and Hannah are friends in their teens/twenties.

THE SET: All that is needed is a sizable wooden cross, some fairy lights and a step-ladder. And I'm assuming that there will be a Christmas tree somewhere in the vicinity.

Sophie is up a ladder putting fairy lights (not yet switched on) on a large wooden cross. She remains focused on this throughout.

Enter Hannah

SOPHIE: Oh, hi

HANNAH: Hi. What you doing?

SOPHIE: I'm doing the Christmas tree. You know? Like you do.

HANNAH: Yeah? You feeling alright?

SOPHIE: I'm fine. Could you hold that for me?

HANNAH: Only it's not a Christmas tree. You do know that don't you?

SOPHIE: Well… depends which way you look at it.

HANNAH: What do you mean? Whichever way you look at it that is most definitely not a Christmas Tree.

SOPHIE: So you say.

HANNAH: So anyone would say, you mentalist!

SOPHIE: You see you could say that this tree has more to do with Christmas than that one has. *(Points to traditional tree)*

HANNAH: *(Groan)* Oh no, you're getting all theological aren't you?

SOPHIE: I'm just saying that, as it happens, this is like the centre of Christianity, whereas that is just an 18th century add-on!

HANNAH: Well maybe, but this is so serious… and Christmas is meant to be fun for heavens sake!

SOPHIE: Oh. (Pause) Is fun the right word?

HANNAH: Well, joyful then! I don't want to think about Jesus dying, do I? I want to think about that sweet little baby… in a manger… and the sheep… and cows… and the little angels…

SOPHIE: Big angels.

HANNAH: *(Cross)* Big angels then! And the star and the Wise Men and all the warm and fuzzy things and you're ruining it!

SOPHIE: Am I?

HANNAH: Yes, you are! I don't like it! Please will you stop!

SOPHIE: OK. *(Gets off ladder)* But the thing is, when you remember the dark side of it all, it makes the light seem…* even more amazing.

*(Switches fairy lights on. Other lights should be dimmed so that the cross stands out. They stand and stare)

HANNAH: *(Subdued)* Amazing Grace.

SOPHIE: Yeah, something like that. *(Folds up ladder and turns to exit)* Got your bagpipes then?

(Exit)

After three, one, two, three…

(Hannah follows, exiting)

THE END

---

* *

TRUE STORY

BACKGROUND: When this was originally performed the entire cast were children, partly because we had some very good child actors at the time: however, there is no reason why some of the more demanding roles shouldn't be taken by adults.

THE CAST: Quentin - a rather theatrical director | Alice - his quiet but organised P.A. | Narrator | Readers | Christmas Fairy* | Angel Gabriel | Mary and Joseph | Turkey* | Pud* | Christmas Cracker* | Innkeepers | Angels | Shepherds | Wise Men and Santa* | Camera operators, Singers, Musicians or backing tracks. *These characters need to be dressed as their name implies!

THE SET: Anything that would help the stage to look like a film studio. It's useful but not essential to have drawback curtains as well. Video cameras (the bigger the better!) trained on the stage can be operated by volunteers who are actually filming!

Blackout

QUENTIN: *(Off-stage)* I can't see them. They're not here.

ALICE: Yes they are. Just keep walking.

Stage lights up

QUENTIN: *(Calling)* Hello! *(They enter)* Oh *(to audience)* there you are! Simply splendid! *(To Alice)* Now what?

ALICE: Welcome.

QUENTIN: Oh yes. Welcome, Ladies and Gentlemen, to our magnificent studio, and this momentous recording. Yes. Er…

ALICE: *(To Quentin)* A few things…

QUENTIN: Just a few things to remind you of. *(To Alice)* What were they?

ALICE: *(Whisper)* Please don't look at the cameras.

QUENTIN: Yes. Please don't look at the cameras.

ALICE: *(Whisper)* Clap when I put this sign up.

QUENTIN: Clap when I put this sign up. What sign? Oh yes. There it is. Oh, and please, no crying babies.

ALICE: Or flash photography.

QUENTIN: Or flash photography. Apart from that have a simply marvellous time! Are we ready studio? Yes. Super.

True Story, take one. Action!

Lights on singers

SONG: *True Story*

Lights on narrator and centre stage

NARRATOR: A long, long time ago, in a land far away, something wonderful happened….

FAIRY: *(Fairy runs on)* Is that my cue? I'm something wonderful!

QUENTIN: *(Loudly)* CUT!! Who the dickens are you?

FAIRY: *(Extremely twee)* Don't you know me? I'm the Christmas fairy. And I've come to bring you all a little bit of Christmas magic. Twinkle, twinkle I'm a star.

ALICE: But you're not in the play.

FAIRY: Oh well, I should be.

QUENTIN: And more to the point, you're not in the story.

FAIRY: So? Who cares?

QUENTIN: AND you're far too PINK.

FAIRY: Well! I'm not staying here to be insulted!

QUENTIN: Good. Get back up your tree then.

(She flounces off stage right)

Where were we?

ALICE: Scene 2.

QUENTIN: Right. O.K. Ready studio? Scene 2. Take 2. Action!

(Tinkling bells)

NARRATOR: A long, long time ago, in a land far away, something wonderful happened which has changed human life forever. The Lord God, Great Creator of the universe, knew that human beings were getting themselves into all kinds of trouble, and he put into action a plan to save them, a plan that he had made before time began. He himself went down to earth and become one of them for a while. And this is how it happened.

(Curtain pulls back to show Mary and Gabriel)

READER: Luke 1:26b-38.
(The scene is mimed. Gabriel leaves stage as reading ends)

SONG: God Has Chosen Me
(Sung by Mary or a soloist)
(Alice holds up the Applause card at the end)

NARRATOR: Nine months later, just before the baby was due to be born, Mary had to go with her husband Joseph to a little town called Bethlehem. The government were taking a census, counting how many people there were in the land. Everyone had to go to the village their ancestors came from.

(During this Joseph appears and takes Mary's hand and leads her off stage left front)

So off they went.

TURKEY AND PUD: (Enter stage right) Stop! Stop! Wait for us!

QUENTIN: CUT! What's all this? What do you think you're doing?

TURKEY: I'm Turkey and he's Pud.

PUD: We're the Christmas dinner!

TURKEY: They can't go without us.

PUD: It's nearly Christmas Day after all.

TURKEY: They'll soon be hungry.

QUENTIN: What are you talking about?!

ALICE: They didn't have turkey and Christmas pudding on the first Christmas Day you know.

QUENTIN: That's just something we do now.

TURKEY: Ohhhhh.

PUD: What? No chipolatas?

ALICE: No chipolatas.

TURKEY: No sprouts?

ALICE: I'm afraid not. No Turkey and Pud either. You're just not in the story. But you can sit there and watch if you like.

PUD: OK then. (They sit)

QUENTIN: Right! Let's get on. Scene 3. Action!!

NARRATOR: When Joseph and Mary arrived in Bethlehem, all the hotels and inns were full up with people who had come for the census. They couldn't find a room anywhere.

(Lots of extras, all shaking their heads. Milling about with them is CRACKER)

SONG: *No Room*
(*Alice holds up Applause card*)

QUENTIN: CUT! I can see you! Come out. Come here.

(*Extras fade away. During this next section of dialogue Mary sits on a hay bale while Joseph sorts out a manger and some hay*)

Now then, explain yourself.

CRACKER: I'm a little cracker I am.

QUENTIN: I can see that.

CRACKER: And I'm ready to go BANG any minute. When does the party start?

ALICE: There isn't one.

CRACKER: What? No Christmas party?

QUENTIN: No!

CRACKER: But what am I going to do?

QUENTIN: You are going to leave the stage - immediately! Security!!

CRACKER: OK.OK. I'm going! (*Exit*)

QUENTIN: (*Shouting*) And no more of this nonsense! This is a true story we're trying to film here.

ALICE: Mind your blood pressure.

QUENTIN: Narrator! Standby studio... action!

NARRATOR: So Mary and Joseph had nowhere to stay.

(*Joseph can keep his back to the audience and screen the manger from sight if you are going for realism! When he stands aside Mary can be seen holding the baby.*)

Joseph found some bundles of hay and made a bed for Mary and that very night, out under the stars, the baby was born: not in a palace, not in a mansion, not even in a humble hotel. His bed was a feeding trough for animals. This is the true story of how God came to earth.

CAROL: *Away In A Manger (Verse 1 only)*
(*Enter shepherds at end. Shepherds and Gabriel act out the reading*)

READING: *Luke 2:8-14*
(*Angels come on during this*)

SONG: *Glory To God or We Give Glory*
(*Angels drift away at the end of the song*)

READING: *Luke 2:15-20*
(*Shepherds turn to face audience*)

SONG: *Nobody Loves Us*
(*Exit shepherds stage left*)

(*Enter Santa stage right*)

SANTA: Ho-ho-ho. Hello Everyone!

QUENTIN: I don't believe it! CUT!

SANTA: And how are we today?

QUENTIN: What are you doing here?

SANTA: Oh, I wouldn't have missed it for the world.

ALICE: I'm sorry Santa, but you're not in the story.

SANTA: Oh yes I am.

SINGERS: Oh no you're not!

SANTA: Oh yes I am.

SINGERS: Oh no you're not!!

SANTA: Oh yes I am.

SINGERS: Oh no you're not!!!

SANTA: Well maybe I'm not, but you can't have Christmas without me. I've got the presents.

EVERYONE: (*gasp*)

ALICE: Maybe. But you haven't got the best present.

SANTA: I don't know what you mean. What IS the best present?

ALICE: (*Goes to crib and picks up Baby Jesus*) It's Jesus, of course.

(*Pause*)

QUENTIN:	Santa, please. Sit down there while we finish the recording.
SANTA:	Well… if I must.
QUENTIN:	One more time studio. Are we ready? Action!

(Quiet music)

READING: *Matthew 2:1-11 (Instrumental over. During reading and narration the Wise Men enter and process to manger)*

NARRATOR:	The gifts which the Wise Men brought all had special meanings. Gold was for majesty, for Jesus the King. Frankincense was for Jesus who is worshipped as God, and Myrrh was for suffering, because when Jesus grew up he died on a cross so that everyone could be a friend of God.

SONG: *Everybody Come Now*
(During this, after the Kings bow down, everybody else gathers round facing the crib and bows down as well, including Santa et al)

CAROL: *O Come, Let Us Adore Him*

QUENTIN:	CUT! That's a wrap. Thank you everybody. Phew! We got there in the end.
CHRISTMAS FAIRY:	Boo Hoo.
QUENTIN:	What's the matter now?
CHRISTMAS FAIRY:	Boo hoo. I'm sad because Jesus died.
ALICE:	Well you needn't be, because he came back to life again. That's in the Easter Sunday Special!!
CHRISTMAS FAIRY:	Oh good! Ple-e-e-ase can I be in it!
CRACKER:	Now can we have a party?
QUENTIN:	Oh, alright then!

(Party poppers etc)

SONG: *It's the Greatest Story*

THE END

* *

WONDERFUL

BACKGROUND: This is written for an all-age cast. It was originally performed in the round.

THE CAST: Prophets, 1, 2 and 3 played by adult men* | Matt, Mark, Luke, John, Sarah, Rebecca, Simon, Peter - all children | Mary, a teenage girl and Joseph, late teens/twenties | Angel Gabriel, non-speaking but has to be a tall and impressive man in an impressive costume (in the Bible angels are always impressive!) | Bethlehem villagers, any age* | Shepherd Boy | Amos, Seth, Jesse, Ben - shepherds played by adult men* | Three Wise men, one is a speaking part, played by adults* | Luke and John as grown men*
*Some of the men could play more than one character, e.g. prophets could be shepherds as well.
Singers and musicians/backing tracks.

THE SET: As this was played in the round we didn't have a set as such. There were two opposite entrances to the central acting area which I have called Side A and Side B, and there was a small raised area of staging for the shepherds scene close to the entrance at Side A. You would need a toy chariot on wheels (wooden if possible!), a makeshift shelter big enough to accommodate Mary, and a manger. We hung a spotlight to shine directly down over the manger area.

Loud drum roll
Lights up on central space

Prophets come on one by one from opposite sides, sometimes crossing over each other. They walk swiftly and speak loudly. This should be a dynamic beginning!

PROPHET 1: Thunder in the desert! Get ready for God's arrival! Make the road straight and smooth, a highway fit for our God. Fill in the valleys, level off the hills, smooth out the ruts, clear out the rocks. Then God's bright glory will shine and everyone will see it. O yes, just as he has said.*

PROPHET 2: He won't shout or strut up and down the streets. He won't brush aside the bruised and broken. He won't disregard the small and insignificant but he'll steadily and firmly put things right. He won't tire out and give up. He wont be stopped until he's finished his work - to set things right on earth.*

PROPHET 3: Look!!... The people who walked in darkness have seen a great light. For those who lived in a land of deep shadows - light... great sunbursts of light!! For a child has been born... for us! The gift of a son... for us! The government of the whole world will be in his hands. He'll be called 'Wonderful, Counsellor, Mighty God, Everlasting Father, Prince of Peace.*

PROPHET 1: *(Comes back in, stands and delivers his line and then ducks back out)*
Watch for this! A girl who is a virgin will conceive and bear a son and call him Immanuel; that means... God with us.*

Lights on singers
SONG: *Messiah*

As song ends enter LUKE, MARK, MATT from Side A running, LUKE first. Enter MARY from Side B with broom, sweeping. Boys run right past her.

MARY: Careful!! Mind my rubbish pile.

LUKE: Sorry Mary.

MARY: I forgive you.

LUKE: *(To Mark)* Anyway, I won.

MARK: No you didn't!

* These passages are from Isaiah in The Message Bible

(Enter John Side A, with toy chariot)

MATT: It was a draw!

(Sees John with chariot)

Woah! What's that?

(Walks over)

Where did you get it?

JOHN: It's mine.

MATT: How come?

JOHN: Joseph gave it to me. He said it was cluttering up his workshop.

MARY: Joseph made it did he?

(Sarah and Rebecca wander in)

JOHN: Yeah. It's a proto something or other. He wants to sell them to the Romans.

LUKE: Yeah. Charge them loads of money.

SARAH: What is it?

MARK: It's a chariot, stupid.

MARY: Mark!

REBECCA: Oh. It's a bit small for a soldier.

JOHN: No. Not for grown up Romans! Children.

SARAH: Oh. Like a toy for them you mean?

MATT: No, no. Not a toy exactly. Well, not for small children.

MARK: Or girls.

REBECCA: That's not fair.

LUKE: We can use it for fighting practice.

JOHN: Smash the Romans!

LUKE/MARK/MATT: Smash the Romans, yeah!

LUKE: Then when the Messiah comes we'll be ready to fight.

ALL BOYS: Yeah!

MARY: When the Messiah comes… who knows what will happen? In the meantime… shouldn't you be at school by now? Look how high the sun is. Go on. Shoo.

JOHN: What shall I do with this?

MARY: I'll take care of it.

JOHN: Don't let them *(Pointing at girls)* play with it.

MARY: Alright then. *(The boys exit)*

SARAH: I wish I could go to school.

REBECCA: So do I. It's boring being a girl.

MARY: But you can learn if you really want to.

SARAH: How?

MARY: You can listen carefully to the Torah and the Rabbis. Ask your parents about our history. That's what I do. Wait till you hear what God has done for us.

REBECCA: I can't wait.

MARY: And it isn't all written in scrolls anyway! Look at the sky and the fields and the flowers and the birds! He made them. They tell you how wonderful he is. Why don't you get out there and play?

SARAH: Good idea Mary. *(To Rebecca)* Shall we play hide and seek?

REBECCA: O.K. I'll hide.

(She runs off, Side A)

SARAH: 1, 2, 3, 4, 5, 6, 7, 8, 9, 10. Ready or not here I come.

(She begins to run off but hearing a very loud noise behind her she turns, half hiding, to look back)

LOUD synthesiser noise as Angel Gabriel appears from Side B. As Mary sees angel she is transfixed, eventually falling to her knees as the music gets louder. No dialogue but it is obvious that there is something being communicated. Then the music begins to fade, the angel steps back a few paces, turns and leaves. Sarah timidly approaches Mary, who is still kneeling

SARAH: What was that?

MARY: *(In shock)* That was an angel, I think. Yes, definitely an angel.

SARAH: Why? What did he want?

MARY: Well… He… he wanted to tell me something.

SARAH: What?

REBECCA: *(Comes running in)* Where've you been, Sarah? I've been waiting for ages.

SARAH: Something's happened. You'll never guess! We've seen an angel?

REBECCA: What?

SARAH: An angel! It was standing there, in front of Mary! Honestly! It was!!

REBECCA: What was it like?

SARAH: It was… big, and shiny and quite scary… Quick Rebecca. Let's tell the others.

They run off, Side A, and bring other girls back with them. Mary stands with her hands clasped under her chin and her eyes closed as the song starts. During the song the girls form a circle round Mary and do a simple dance

SONG/DANCE: *Magnificat*
(Sung by choir soloist)
(As the song ends enter Joseph from Side A. The children drift off apart from Sarah and Rebecca who hang around behind Joseph)

JOSEPH: Hey. What's all the noise about?

MARY: Joseph!

JOSEPH: That's my name. *(Playfully)* And you would be?

MARY: Don't be silly Joseph. Listen. I've got something to tell you.

JOSEPH: Hey! That's my chariot. What's it doing there?

MARY: Oh, I'm looking after it while John's at school. Joseph, I'm trying to tell you something. It's, er, it's important you see. Erm. Well… It's like this… I'm going to have a baby.

JOSEPH: Yes of course you are, we're going to have loads of children - one day.

MARY: No. Yes. I mean, no. I mean, soon, and it's not your baby!

JOSEPH: Not mine? Is this a joke?

MARY: No. You see, I know this sounds weird but I'm going to have… God's child, a child by the Holy Spirit.

JOSEPH: Because if it's a joke it isn't funny.

MARY: No Joseph, I'm serious. I was told, just now, by… an angel.

JOSEPH: Mary! You're talking like a mad woman!

MARY: Yes. I know how it must sound.

SARAH: It's true. There was an angel. I saw it.

JOSEPH: Sarah. You wouldn't lie about this would you? It's really important.

SARAH: I'm not lying. There was an angel. I saw it. I was scared!

JOSEPH: *(To Mary)* We need to talk about this. Privately.

(He turns and walks off and Mary follows him.)

REBECCA: Joseph's mad.

SARAH: I know! He doesn't believe her.

(Enter boys heading for chariot)

JOHN: Phew. It's still there. Come on, let's try it out. Smash the Romans!!!

MARK: Smash them to bits!

REBECCA: You'll never guess….

SARAH: Shh. Maybe better not.

MATT: What? What are you on about?

SARAH: Never mind. Can we play too?

LUKE: Well you can be pretend horses and pull it if you want but you're not having a ride in it.

GIRLS: Tut/Aw.

LUKE: *(As they exit)* Maybe after we've been to Bethlehem.

REBECCA: But that's months and months away!

JOHN: What can we do? Our hands are tied.

SARAH: No they're not!

REBECCA: You're just mean, that's all. Anyway, *(exiting)* we know something you don't know.

(Stage empties)

Music of O Bethlehem with only the words O Bethlehem actually sung.
Enter a few adults walking back and forth in a busy fashion, carrying this and that, bundles of blankets etc.
Over the music…

VOICE OFF-STAGE: *(Into a microphone)* O Bethlehem, David's Bethlehem! Small you may be, but you will be the birthplace of my King, who is alive from everlasting ages past.

(Music fades)

Enter two boys, carrying chair. One stands on it, peering into distance

SIMON: Can you see them?

PETER: There's lots of dust but there's someone just coming now. It might be them. I wonder what they look like?

SIMON: They probably look like us! We are relatives after all.

PETER: We might never see them again after this. Nazareth's days and days from here.

SIMON: Yeah but we might see them in Jerusalem!

PETER: Sure *(Luke and John enter with chariot)* Here's someone. Hi.

LUKE & JOHN: Hi.

SIMON: Are you Luke and John by any chance?

LUKE: Yeah. How did you know? The rest of the people from our village are behind.

SIMON: Oh right. Well, we're your kind of cousins. Er, yeah. So, welcome to Bethlehem.

JOHN: Thanks.

PETER: What's that?

JOHN: It's a chariot.

LUKE: We use it for playing Smash the Romans.

JOHN: Smash the Romans!!

SIMON & PETER: Shhhhhh!

LUKE: What?

SIMON: You have to be careful round here. The Romans don't like that sort of thing… and they have spies. Sometimes they kill people if they don't like them. They nail them up by their hands till they're dead.

JOHN: Urgh.

PETER: But we can still play with it if we're careful. Do you want to see where we live? It's crazy here. So many people have come for the census. We're all squashed in one room.

SIMON: Where are you staying?

LUKE: Don't know.

(They move off to organ end)

SIMON: My Mum says everywhere is
               full up already. You can sleep
               on our roof if you like, we all
               could.

ALL: Yeah!!

SHEPHERD BOY: *(Walks past in opposite
               direction)* Hello.

PETER: Don't talk to him. He's a
               shepherd boy. Nobody likes
               shepherds. Come on.

SONG: *No Room*
*(During this song some adults plus Mary and
Joseph arrive and engage in conversation
with Bethlehem villagers. Lots of shaking of
heads)*

JOSEPH: I knew this would happen. I
               knew it. I'm going to try to rig
               something up for you.

MARY: Be quick Joseph.

JOSEPH: Alright, alright. *(Suddenly
               worried)* What do you mean?

MARY: The pains have started.

JOSEPH: Oh no. Not now. Not here. Why
               here? What? What are you
               doing Lord?

MARY: It's the prophecy. I told you.
               Has to be Bethlehem.

JOSEPH: In the middle of the street?
               Right. You sit there. Keep
               calm.

*(He erects a shelter over Mary which
conceals her from view)*

               This might not be much but it's
               the best I can do in the
               circumstances.

(Music comes up)

               Good thing I had the
               forethought to bring all

this. Not many men would have
been that organised I can tell
you, are you alright?

*(Puts his head under the covering and out
again)*

               O flip. Is there a midwife
               anywhere?

(Dives back under the cover)

               Don't panic.

*Lights down on Mary and Joseph. Lights up
on singers*

SONG: *O Bethlehem*
*Lights down on singers. Overhead spotlight
on Joseph*

*Joseph emerges holding baby, wanders to a
spot right under a light*

JOSEPH: So. Here you are then. I hope
               it's alright to hold you,
               I mean, I hope I don't get
               struck by a thunderbolt or
               anything. *(Pause)* Mm. So far, so
               good. Thing is, you look… just
               like one of us, as it happens,
               and you'll probably need me,
               for a while, anyway, so. Yeah.
               (Pause) Look up there. Those
               twinkling things. They're
               called stars. Oh, you probably
               know that already, don't you?
               You probably know what
               they're called as well, come to
               think of it. Anyway, there's
               hundreds of them up there
               tonight, twinkling away.
               There's a big one, right over
               our heads. How about that eh?

Keep light on Joseph
SONG: *Shine On, Jesus*
(Best as a child solo)

Lights on shepherds.
Shepherds on raised platform, Side A.

AMOS: Clear night. Lotta stars. Goin'
               cold I reckon.

SETH: Yep.

33

AMOS:	Gonna light a nice big fire in a minute.
SETH:	Did you count all the sheep in then?
AMOS:	I did. Good thing one of us can count.
JESSE:	What you talking about? I can count.
AMOS:	Yea. Only up to ten though. And we got hundreds of sheep.
SETH:	He's good with his hands though, our Jess.
BEN:	Tell you what, I'm glad I'm not down town tonight.
JESSE:	Me too. It's murder down there. You can't move for visitors.
BEN:	People campin' on the streets they are.
AMOS:	Innkeepers doin' all right though.
BEN:	Well it's an ill wind blows nobody any good.
SETH:	Speaking of which, there's a breeze getting' up. Feels a bit strange I reckon. Something in the air.

(Synthesiser noise begins, grows and white light comes up on stage)

AMOS:	I know what you mean. And the sky's getting lighter. Where's the moon? I can't see the moon. Where's the light coming from?
JESSE:	What's happening? It's not an earthquake is it? O God save us.

(Loud synthesiser noise. Big chords. Angels run on and surround shepherds, Gabriel with his arms raised stands in front of them with his back to the audience)

SONG: *Glory To God*
(Music continues quietly)

GABRIEL:	*(Voice off-stage over P.A.?)* Don't be afraid! I'm bringing you wonderful news, for you and for everyone, all over the world. A Saviour has just been born, in Bethlehem, a Saviour who is Messiah and Lord. This is how you will know. You will find a baby, wrapped in a blanket, and lying in a manger.

SONG: *Glory To God*
(During this Joseph goes off and comes back carrying a manger. Music fades and angelic choir exit)

AMOS:	*(Gobsmacked)* We've seen angels.
SETH:	We've gotta go. Quick.
JESSE:	Can't all go.
BEN:	You stay then.
AMOS:	We'll be straight back.

(They run off, maybe round the outside and back in at the opposite entrance, if possible)

Lights up on Joseph and Mary; Joseph carrying manger.

JOSEPH:	Will this be alright for now? It's all I could find.
MARY:	What would my Mother say? No. I'm kidding. It'll do fine. It doesn't smell too bad.

(Lays child in manger)

	Bless him.

(Luke, John, Simon and Peter run in noisily, with chariot)

JOSEPH:	Shhhh. The baby's asleep.
LUKE:	What baby? Oh. Is it Mary's baby?

(They cluster round)

JOHN:	Boy or girl?
JOSEPH:	Boy of course.
JOHN:	Yeah!

LUKE: Yeah. Well. Good. Come on then.

(They run off)

MARY: *(After them, maternally)* Shouldn't you be in bed by now?

(Shepherds come running in, stop suddenly at manger and stare. Pause)

JOSEPH: Er, Good Evening. Can I help you?

AMOS: Evening. Yes. Well. No. Well. I was just wondering. You've got a baby there, all wrapped up like… in a manger.

JOSEPH: Yes.

AMOS: Well, that's unusual that is. You don't see that every day.

JOSEPH: Well it's all I could find. We're not from these parts.

SETH: Tell him Amos. Go on.

AMOS: Well it's like this see, we, you won't believe it but… we just seen… angels.

BEN: Angels. Yeah. We did. Honest.

SETH: Millions of 'em. Big ones, little ones.

BEN: Yeah.

AMOS: And one of them spoke to us.

SETH: Yeah he did.

MARY: What was he like?

BEN: Oh. Big he was.

MARY: And was he very bright and shining?

AMOS: Bright and shining. Yeah. How do you know?

MARY: Oh *(shyly)*… he came to me once.

SETH: He said a Saviour's been born here tonight. Is this… is this him?

AMOS: Course it is.

(Kneels down, followed by the others)

BEN: What's his name, if you don't mind my asking?

JOSEPH: It's Jesus.

SETH: Jesus. Well now. A Saviour. Little tiny thing.

AMOS: And we're here looking at him. I can't believe it. We're only shepherds after all. Fancy them angels bothering to tell us.

MARY: The Lord would have told them to I expect.

AMOS: Well. It's a mystery to me. Why would… I dunno. *(Pause)*

BEN: Better be getting back to the sheep then.

SETH: Yeah. Thanks for lettin' us have a look like.

(They bow and go off)

AMOS: Wait till I tell the wife.

SETH: I'm telling everyone, I am.

(Shepherds head back to the raised platform and sing this with singers).

SONG: *Nobody Loves Us*

(Shepherds exit and Boys come racing in again)

JOSEPH: Are you still up?

LUKE: *(To Mary)* John says that Joseph says that you said that your baby is the Messiah.

JOSEPH: John, I told you it was a secret.

JOHN: Sorry.

MARY: It's alright. Everyone will know sooner or later.

JOHN: It's true then. And the bit about the angel, that's true as well?

MARY:	It's all true. It's strange but it's... wonderful. And it's happening to us. *(Pause)*
LUKE:	So, anyway, when we're back in Nazareth, and he's growing up, I can teach him how to fight!
JOHN:	Yeah!
MARY:	He might not want to fight. Have you thought of that?
LUKE:	Of course he will!
JOHN:	What else would he do?
MARY:	Well, I expect he'll do... whatever God tells him to. And that might surprise us.
JOSEPH:	Boys. Mary needs to rest. Scoot off to where you're staying. We'll see you tomorrow.
LUKE:	O.K. then. *(To cradle)* Good night. Messiah. *(Boys exit)*
JOSEPH:	Lets try and make you comfortable.

Lights all go way down except for spotlight over manger.

SONG: *Wonderful*

As the song fades a figure approaches Joseph in the half-light. Mary should stay out of sight at first. Conversation is half-whispered.

BALTHAZAR:	Excuse me. Sorry to disturb you. This might seem strange but I'm looking for child, a newborn, the King of the Jews. Have you any idea where he might be?
JOSEPH:	What do you mean exactly?
BALTHAZAR:	*(Patiently, slowly)* I'm looking for a child, newly born. I believe him to be the King of the Jews.
JOSEPH:	I see. And you are?
BALTHAZAR:	I am a scholar Sir. From a long way East of here. My friends

	and I have travelled many miles. We followed this star. This one here. *(Pointing up)* And here it is, right over you, right over this child.
JOSEPH:	And what do you want from him? *(Mary comes out)*
BATHAZAR:	We want nothing but to see him, to worship him.
MARY:	You are welcome Sir. This is the child you're searching for. This is our Messiah.
BALTHAZAR:	Oh. I knew it! I knew it!! Melchior, Gaspar, come! He is here. The King of the Jews!

(Melchior and Gaspar enter)

MARY:	Not just the King of the Jews. *(Music)* His name will be Wonderful! Counsellor, Mighty God, Everlasting Father, Prince of Peace. And he will reign forever and ever. And one day, every knee will bow to him, in heaven and on earth.

SONG: *Everybody Come Now*
(During this the Wise Men cluster round the baby, and they open gifts to give to him)

The music should move seamlessly into this next song.

CAROL: *O Come, Let Us Adore Him*
(During verse 2 and 3 of this song Mary and Joseph and Wise Men walk out. Lights dim. Shelter and manger are removed)

Music: e.g. Chime Bars to indicate the passage of time.
Lights up on centre
Luke and John are in their thirties/forties. They cross paths at the centre, John with the wooden chariot.

JOHN:	Look what I just found.
LUKE:	Well I'll be blowed! After all this time! Still in good nick tho'.
JOHN:	He was a good carpenter, old Joseph.

LUKE:	That he was.	**JOHN:**	He fought for us.

LUKE: That he was.

JOHN: Remember what we used to play with this?

LUKE: (Smiles) Smash the Romans!

JOHN: Yeah. He never did though, did he?

LUKE: Who? Jesus? No. Blessed them, as it happens!

JOHN: We had him all wrong. Thank goodness.

LUKE: We thought we might fight for him, but in the end…

JOHN: He fought for us.

LUKE: Yeah. Died for us. A Saviour. And we saw him

JOHN: With our own eyes!!!

LUKE: (Really loud, joyous shout, holding into music) HALLELUJAH!!

(No pause. Straight in. Unaccompanied. A strong singer needs to start it.)

CAROL: Gaudete
(The rest of the cast come on briskly and make a circle facing outwards. The song is repeated a few times and ends with a shouted 'Gaudete!!')

THE END

* *

All Wrapped Up

♩ = 112

Judy MacKenzie Dunn

All wrapped up and ly - ing in a man - ger, ba - by Je - sus,

when he was born. All wrapped up and ly - ing in a man - ger,

he's God's pre sent for ev - 'ry-one, he's God's pre sent for ev - 'ry -

one.

Angel Voices

Judy MacKenzie Dunn

1. If we could see through an - gels' eyes, ___ if we could fly on
2. If we could hear what an - gels hear, ___ if we could know what

an - gels' wings, ___ we'd look down from a - bove the skies ___ and see a -
an - gels know, ___ our song would rise to hea - vens door ___ and touch the

1. maz - ing ___ things.
earth be -

2. low.

An - gel voi - ces, al - ways sing - ing, al - ways sing - ing, round your throne.

An - gel voi - ces al - ways bring - ing songs of praise, songs of love,

songs of praise to you a - lone.

Everybody Come Now

♩ = 160

Judy MacKenzie Dunn

Ev-'ry-bo-dy come now, ev-'ry-bo-dy bow down,

ev-'ry-bo-dy bow down to the King.___ Ev-'ry-bo-dy

Wor-ship Je-sus,___ King of glo-ry,___ God most

ho-ly,___ wor-ship him. Wor-ship Je-sus,___

Man of Suf-fer-ing,___ e-ver-last-ing Lord and

King._____ Ev-'ry-bo-dy Wor-ship

Glory To God

Steadily ♪ = 112

Judy MacKenzie Dunn

Chorus

Glo-ry to God, glo-ry to God, glo-ry to God in the high-est.

Glo-ry to God, glo-ry to God, glo-ry to God in the high-est.____ And

Verse

peace on earth, peace on earth to those on whom his fa-vour rests.

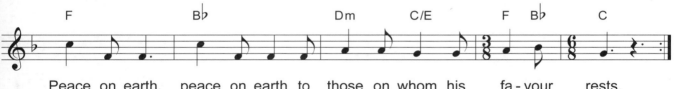

Peace on earth, peace on earth to those on whom his fa-vour rests.

Coda

high - est.____ Glo-ry to God.

God Has Chosen Me

Moderately ♩ = 96

Judy MacKenzie Dunn

1. God has cho - sen me,_____ he has called me by my
   cho - sen me,_____ he has called me by my

name. It's a my - ste-ry,_____ on - ly hea - ven can ex -
name. It's a my - ste-ry,_____ on - ly hea - ven can ex -

plain. Here I am, an or - di - na - ry girl,
plain. Here I am, the ser - vant of the Lord,

and I'm the one to bring his light in - to the world. 2. God has
let it be to me ac - cord - ing to his

word._____

Great Big Star

♩ = 112

Judy MacKenzie Dunn

It's The Greatest Story Ever Told

Judy MacKenzie Dunn

Love Is Coming

♩ = 56

Judy MacKenzie Dunn

Hey now, hush now, lift your eyes,— love is com-ing; hey now, hush now, love is— near.

love is— near. Hey now, hush now, turn a-round,— love is com-ing;

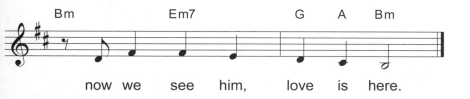

now we see him, love is here.

Magnificat

♩. = 74

Judy MacKenzie Dunn

Solo E   E/G#   F#m/A   F#m   E   E/G#

1. My heart is full of praise to God, my joy in him is
2. The ge - ne - ra - tions still to come will lis - ten to my
3. For he, the migh - ty, ho - ly one is awe - some in his

C#m   B   A   B   E   C#m

grow - ing, for he has not for - got - ten me, but
st - ory; the Lord has done great things for me be -
po - wer, and faith - ful to his pro - mi - ses for

F#m   A   B E   **All** A   B

gi - ven me his bles - sing. For he has not for -
cause of his great mer - cy. The Lord has done great
e - ver and for e - ver. And faith - ful to his

Last time repeat this section 3 times

E   C#m   F#m   A   B E

got - ten me, but gi - ven me his bles - sing.
things for me be - cause of his great mer - cy.
pro - mi - ses for e - ver and for e - ver.

Messiah

Moderately ♩ = 124

Judy MacKenzie Dunn

Verse Dm / B♭

1. Stand-ing on the watch-tower, walk-ing on the high ground,
2. Steal-ing through the sha-dows, hid-ing from the moon-light,

C / Gm Asus4 A

look-ing all a-round you. can you see a-ny-one?
lis-ten-ing for foot-steps, is there a-ny-one there? How

Dm / B♭

Watch-ing the ho-ri-zon for a-ny-thing that's mov-ing,
e-ver long it's tak-ing, there is no mis-tak-ing,

C / Gm Asus4 A **Chorus** Gm

could be a-ny day now, yes, we know he will come. Mes-si-ah,— Mes-
when we find Mes-si-ah we will live with-out fear.

Dm A7 Dm Em7 D7/F♯ Gm Dm

si-ah,— our Shep-herd,— our Sa-viour; Mes-si-ah,— Mes-si-ah,— our

A Dm Gm Dm A

con-quer-ing King. Mes-si-ah,— Mes-si-ah,— our Migh-ty— Re-

Dm Em7 D7/F♯ Gm Dm A7 **(Fine)** Dm

deem-er; Mes-si-ah,— Mes-si-ah,— we're wait-ing— for him.

Gm Dm A7 Dm **D.C. al Fine**

No Room!

♩ = 140

Judy MacKenzie Dunn

No room, no room, no room. No room, no room, no room. No room, no room, no

room. No room, no room, no room. There's just no room! No

room, no room, no room. No room, no room, no room. No room, no room, no

room. No room, no room, no room. There's just no room! (No)

Nobody Loves Us

Judy MacKenzie Dunn

♩ = 114

No-bo-dy loves us,— ev-'ry-bo-dy hates us;— no-bo-dies like us.

Peo-ple hold their no-ses,— 'cos we don't smell of ro-ses;— no-bo-dies like

us. Shep-herds, they say— are smel-ly and poor,— but we don't

care a-ny-more,— be-cause we've seen mil-lions of an - gels, and

we've heard mil-lions of an - gels, and they had good news for us,

for us: no-bo - dies like us!

O Bethlehem

Shine On, Jesus

♩ = 98

Judy MacKenzie Dunn

Verse

The sky is full of stars to - night, and one of them is shin - ing bright, it's shin - ing down with all its might o - ver Beth - le - hem.

Chorus

Shine on, Je - sus, shine on, Je - sus, shine on Je - sus, shine. The

shine. shine.

Shine

Judy MacKenzie Dunn

True Story

♩ = 104

Judy MacKenzie Dunn

1. Here is a sto - ry,___ true sto-ry,___ the most a - maz-ing___
2. This is a part of___ his sto-ry:___ Jo - seph and Ma - ry,___

true sto - ry;___ out of the pa - ges___ of hi - sto-ry,___
long jour-ney.___ mil - lions of an - gels___ and one ba - by,___

we tell the sto - ry__ of Je - sus, we tell the sto - ry__ of Je-sus.
we tell the sto - ry__ of Je - sus, we tell the sto - ry__ of

Je - sus, some call him Sa-viour, Je - sus, some call him Friend,

D.C. (v.1) al Fine

Je - sus, some say Mes - si - ah, King of all kings.___

Welcome

Judy MacKenzie Dunn

1. Wel - come one and wel - come all.
2. God, the Lord of hea - ven and earth,
3. Ne - ver was, since time be - gan,

Wel - come to my Ma - ster's hall.
comes to us by hu - man birth;
such a tale of God and man;

Sit ye down and sup ye well,
he, the King of high re - nown,
hum - ble souls from far and near,

hear the tale that we do tell.
lays a - side his gol - den crown.
such a won - der now shall hear.

We Sing Glory

Judy MacKenzie Dunn

What Can We Bring

Judy MacKenzie Dunn

Wonderful

♩ = 86

Judy MacKenzie Dunn

Some - one o - pened hea - ven's door to - night,____

hea - ven's mu - sic fills the air to - night.____

Love comes down, mak-ing the earth his home, mak-ing our

world his own, won - der - ful.____ Won - der - ful.____

Won - der - ful.____ Won - der - ful.____

Lyrics

All Wrapped Up

All wrapped up
And lying in a manger
Baby Jesus, when he was born
All wrapped up
And lying in a manger
He's God's present for everyone
He's God's present for everyone

Angel Voices

If we could see
Through angels' eyes
If we could fly on angels' wings
We'd look down
From above the skies
And see amazing things

If we could hear what angels hear
If we could know what angels know
Our song would rise to heavens door
And touch the earth below

Angel voices, always singing
Always singing, round your throne
Angel voices always bringing
Songs of praise to you alone

Everybody Come Now

Everybody come now
Everybody bow down
Everybody bow down
To the King
To the King

Worship Jesus, King of glory
God most holy, worship him
Worship Jesus, Man of Suffering
Everlasting Lord and King

Glory To God

Glory to God, glory to God
Glory to God in the highest
Glory to God, glory to God
Glory to God in the highest
And peace on earth
Peace on earth
For those on whom
His favour rests
And peace on earth
Peace on earth
For those on whom
His favour rests

God Has Chosen Me

God has chosen me
He has called me by my name
It's a mystery
Only heaven can explain
Here I am, an ordinary girl
And I'm the one to bring
His light into the world

God has chosen me
He has called me by my name
It's a mystery
Only heaven can explain
Here I am, the servant of the Lord
Let it be to me
According to his word

Great Big Star

Solo
I'm gonna be a great big star
Just you wait and see
People will come from near and far
For just one look at me
I'm gonna have my name in lights
Higher than a Christmas tree
I'm gonna be a great big star
Just you wait and see

All
She's gonna be a great big star
Just you wait and see
People will come from near and far

Solo
For just one look at me

All
She's gonna have her name in lights
Higher than a Christmas tree

Solo
I'm gonna be a great big star
Just you wait and see

It's The Greatest Story Ever Told

It's the greatest story ever told
It's the greatest news
We've ever heard
It's the biggest wonder
In the whole wide world
That God came down to earth

He came down to us
He was one of us
And he lived and died
So we could live for ever
He came down to us
He was one of us
Came to live with us
So we could live with him

It's the greatest story ever told
It's the greatest news
We've ever heard
It's the biggest wonder
In the whole wide world
That God came down to earth

Love Is Coming

Hey now, hush now
Lift your eyes, love is coming
Hey now, hush now, love is near
Hey now, hush now
Turn around, love is coming
Now we see him, love is here

Magnificat

Solo
My heart is full of praise to God
My joy in him is growing
For he has not forgotten me
But given me his blessing

All
For he has not forgotten me
But given me his blessing

Solo
The generations still to come
Will listen to my story
The Lord has done great things for me
Because of his great mercy

All
The Lord has done great things for me
Because of his great mercy

Solo
For he the mighty, holy one
Is awesome in his power
And faithful to his promises
For ever and for ever

All
He's faithful to his promises
For ever and for ever

Messiah

Standing on the watchtower
Walking on the high ground
Looking all around you
Can you see anyone?
Watching the horizon
For anything that's moving
Could be any day now
Yes we know he will come

Messiah, Messiah
Our Shepherd, our Saviour
Messiah, Messiah, our conquering King
Messiah, Messiah
Our Mighty Redeemer
Messiah, Messiah, we're waiting for him

Stealing through the shadows
Hiding from the moonlight
Listening for footsteps
Is there anyone there?
However long it's taking
There is no mistaking
When we find Messiah
We will live without fear

Nobody Loves Us

Nobody loves us
Everybody hates us
Nobodies like us
People hold their noses
'Cos we don't smell of roses
Nobodies like us

Shepherds, they say
Are smelly and poor
But we don't care anymore
Because we've seen
Millions of angels
And we've heard
Millions of angels
And they had good news for us
Nobodies like us

No Room

No Room, no room, no room
No Room, no room, no room
No Room, no room, no room

No Room, no room, no room
No Room, no room, no room
No Room, no room, no room

No Room, no room, no room
No Room, no room, no room
No Room, no room

There's just no room!

O Bethlehem

O Bethlehem
You can hold your head up high
O Bethlehem
You'll go down in history
To you a child is born
To you a son is given
To you the King has come
Lord of all earth and heaven

Shine On, Jesus

The sky is full of stars tonight
And one of them is shining bright
It's shining down with all its might
Over Bethlehem
Shine on, Jesus
Shine on, Jesus
Shine on, Jesus, shine

Shine

Let me be the kind of star
That leads the way to where you are
I want to shine, I want to shine
For you, Jesus

As I look into your face
May I reflect your loveliness
I want to shine, I want to shine
For you

Even when my light has gone
You'll keep shining on and on and on
Brighter than the moon, the stars
The sun, eternally

Let me be the kind of star
That leads the way to where you are
I want to shine, I want to shine
For you

True Story

Here is a story, true story
The most amazing - true story
Out of the pages of - history
We tell the story of Jesus

This is a part of his story
Joseph and Mary, long journey
Millions of angels, one baby
We tell the story of Jesus
We tell the story of

Jesus, some call him Saviour
Jesus, some call him Friend
Jesus, some say Messiah
King of all kings
Here is a story, true story
The most amazing - true story
Out of the pages of - history
We tell the story of Jesus
We tell the story of Jesus

Welcome

Welcome one and welcome all
Welcome to my Master's hall
Sit ye down and sup ye well
Hear the tale that we do tell

God, the Lord of heaven and earth
Comes to us by human birth
He, the King of high renown
Lays aside his golden crown

Never was, since time began
Such a tale of God and man
Humble souls from far and near
Such a wonder now shall hear

We Sing Glory

We sing glory, we sing glory
We sing glory to God in the highest
We sing glory, we sing glory
We sing glory to God Most High

What Can We Bring?

What can we bring?
To you who have everything?
What can we bring
To the King of kings?
What can we offer
The Lord our Creator
Maker of all good things?

Gold for your Majesty
Incense for holiness
Myrrh for your suffering
Hearts full of love for you
Lives that bring joy to you
These are our offering
To the King, to the king

Wonderful

Someone opened heavens door tonight
Heavens music fills the air tonight
Love comes down
Making the earth his home
Making our world his own
Wonderful

* *

Additional Backing Tracks

Away In A Manger (Verse 1 only)

MARTIN LUTHER | JOHN THOMAS MCFARLAND | JAMES RAMSEY MURRAY | © PUBLIC DOMAIN

Away in a manger, no crib for a bed
The little Lord Jesus laid down his sweet head
The stars in the bright sky looked down where he lay
The little Lord Jesus, asleep on the hay

Gaudete (Trad)

© PUBLIC DOMAIN

Gaudete, gaudete
Christus est natus
Ex Maria Virgine
Gaudete

God Rest Ye Merry Gentlemen (Verse 2 only)

AUTHOR UNKNOWN | © PUBLIC DOMAIN

From God our Heavenly Father
A blessed angel came
And unto certain shepherds
Brought tidings of the same
How that in Bethlehem was born
The Son of God by name

O tidings of comfort and joy
Comfort and joy
O tidings of comfort and joy

The Saviour Of The World Is Born

WORDS: JUDY MACKENZIE DUNN | © ELEVATION
TUNE: I SAW THREE SHIPS | © PUBLIC DOMAIN

The Saviour of the world is born
This Christmas Day, this Christmas Day
The Saviour of the world is born
This Christmas Day in the morning

Let all creation shout for joy
This Christmas Day, this Christmas Day
Let all creation shout for joy
This Christmas Day in the morning

And we shall sing for evermore
Of Christmas Day, of Christmas Day
And we shall sing for evermore
Of Christmas Day in the morning

O Come Let Us Adore Him

CURTIS MULDER | JON FRANCIS WADE | © PUBLIC DOMAIN

O come, let us adore him
O come, let us adore him
O come, let us adore him
Christ the Lord

For he alone is worthy
For he alone is worthy
For he alone is worthy
Christ the Lord

We'll give you all the glory
We'll give you all the glory
We'll give you all the glory
Christ the Lord

The Angel Gabriel

SABINE BARING-GOULD | © PUBLIC DOMAIN

The angel Gabriel from heaven came
With wings as drifted snow, with eyes as flame
"All hail" said he, "Thou lowly maiden Mary
Most highly favoured lady. Gloria!"

We Three Kings

JOHN HENRY HOPKINS JR | © PUBLIC DOMAIN

We three kings of Orient are
Bearing gifts we traverse afar
Field and fountain, moor and mountain
Following yonder star

O Star of wonder, star of night
Star with royal beauty bright
Westward leading, still proceeding
Guide us to thy Perfect Light

Born a King on Bethlehem's plain
Gold I bring to crown him again
King forever, ceasing never
Over us all to reign

Frankincense to offer have I
Incense owns a Deity nigh
Prayer and praising, all men raising
Worship him, God most high

Myrrh is mine, its bitter perfume
Breathes of life of gathering gloom
Sorrowing, sighing, bleeding, dying
Sealed in the stone-cold tomb

Glorious now behold him arise
King and God and Sacrifice
Alleluia, alleluia
Earth to heav'n replies

*　*